FLOWER
ARRANGING

A simple arrangement of daffodils and daisies is enhanced by antique silver pieces.

FLOWER
ARRANGING

Susan McAffer

Bloomsbury Books
London

Special thanks to Wendy B, Wendy B Flowers.

Published by Harlaxton Publishing Ltd
2 Avenue Road, Grantham, Lincolnshire, NG31 6TA, United Kingdom.
A Member of the Weldon International Group of Companies.

First published in 1992.

This edition published in 1993 by
Bloomsbury Books
an imprint of
The Godfrey Cave Group
42 Bloomsbury Street, London. WC1B 3QJ
under license from Harlaxton Publishing Ltd.

Publishing Manager: Robin Burgess
Project Coordinator: Mary Moody
Editor: Dulcie Andrews
Illustrator: Kathie Baxter Smith
Designed & produced for the publisher by Phillip Mathews Publishers
Produced in Singapore by Imago

British Library Cataloguing-in-Publication data.
A catalogue record for this book is available from the British Library.
Title: Country Crafts Series: Flower Arranging
ISBN:1 85471 146 6

CONTENTS

INTRODUCTION

Through this Country Craft series, it is our hope that you will find satisfaction and enjoyment in learning a new skill. On this occasion, that of flower arranging.

Flowers in the home are always a pleasure. Handling and arranging them will bring many hours of satisfaction. The variety of materials that can be used and the arrangements that can be made are only limited by your imagination. Enhancing a room can often be as simple as placing a few snowdrops in a vase.

The basic steps are outlined in this book to assist you to achieve the look you require.

A glorious display of summer flowers.

GETTING STARTED

THE MATERIALS AVAILABLE to produce flower arrangements are varied and often surprising. A walk in the country or down a garden path can produce leaves, branches and twigs, berries, nuts and grasses in abundance. Even in the middle of winter with a little imagination a pretty arrangement can be completed.

Over the years many so-called rules have been applied to flower arrangements. People, in their wisdom, deemed it inappropriate for one colour to go with another or one type of flower to be used with another. Fortunately today many of these myths have been forgotten. In fact, with the new casual styles – which are the essence of country style – the adage 'anything goes' can, and does, apply.

Formal arrangements have their place, particularly on special occasions. In general, if you try to approach an arrangement in the simplest manner, you will discover that the secret of style lies in its simplicity.

Choosing one flower, picking a bunch from the garden or buying them from a shop is fun. It is not necessary to buy or grow expensive blooms to capture a country style. In fact, simple seasonal material is readily available. Often a single flower, a cluster of ripened seed heads, or a bunch of wild flowers will provide all you need.

Some people have an 'eye for colour' or an instinctive colour sense. You should not hesitate to experiment with different colour combinations. It may be easier to start with arrangements that blend harmoniously with your room decoration. There are many art books that explain the principles of colour and will help you define which colours work particularly well together and which colours can provide dramatic contrast.

Pale pink, cream and pale blue make a lovely combination, as does a selection of gold, yellow and cream. Bright blues and yellows provide a stunning contrast as in a posy of cornflowers and marigolds.

If you want a simple way to check colour combinations before you pick or buy flowers, obtain a full set of sample paint cards from a do-it-yourself shop and use these to help you match objects in your room and to try various combinations together.

When you are finally ready to begin, decide where your arrangement is to be placed. Consider the effect that you are trying to achieve, gather together the materials you want to use and have fun.

Opposite: A basketful of flowers provides a charming arrangement, either inside or on a patio.

Try arrangements in different parts of a room. Flowers do not always have to be on the mantelpiece.

A cottage garden always has something in flower for the house.

Tall stem grass, heliconia and euphorbia make a striking display.

TOOLS AND MATERIALS

IT IS NOT NECESSARY to rush out and buy a whole lot of equipment to complete a wide variety of arrangements successfully. The main purpose of taking the time and effort needed to arrange the material is to show it off in the most effective way possible. Attention should be paid to shape, proportion and colour, as compatibility between flowers, foliage and the container is essential.

On some occasions the vase may be almost as important as the flowers themselves. There are many times, however, when the container is hidden by the arrangement and serves solely as a receptacle to anchor the material and provide a source of water. In these instances, a baking tray can be just as useful as an expensive vase. The reverse may occur when you have only a few blooms, as the container's style and appeal will be paramount and can contribute greatly to the charm of the arrangement.

A flower container does not have to be a vase. The kitchen cupboard will invariably provide a variety of interestingly shaped objects. Jugs, casserole dishes, a soup tureen, mugs, a lidless teapot or even an empty bottle or spaghetti jar can often provide just the shape and size to match the material.

In addition to finding the right container, it can sometimes be necessary to use some florist's aids. The materials which we will outline in this book can be bought from most florist shops or florist's suppliers.

CONTAINERS

Glass

Glass containers vary widely and range from beautifully designed vases to decanters, goblets, fish bowls and medicine or chemistry bottles. Look for shapes which offer a firm, heavy base and, if they are wide-necked, allow room to conceal wire netting under the flowers.

A glass specimen vase can be the ideal container to display a single bloom. Choose one with a firm, solid base which is not too tall, as they can easily topple over. A brandy

Containers come in all shapes and sizes.

Containers in simple shapes and basic colours are the easiest with which to work.

glass can be ideal for a bunch of tiny blooms like violets. Tied lightly together and placed in the centre of the glass, they will look very pretty and will last longer than usual in the moist atmosphere created by the shape of the glass.

Glass must be kept clean and polished. Scrub containers well after use with soapy water, as a spotless vase will reduce the problem of wilting. Watermarks can occur and should be removed regularly, otherwise they could become permanent. A piece of lemon dipped in salt will help to remove stains.

Ceramics

From Art Deco to modern or antique, from fine porcelain to rough pottery, the variety is endless. Ceramics are usually easy to use and weighty enough not to topple over once an arrangement is in place. They offer the advantage that no stems can be seen and they obscure wire, florist's foam or any other fixatives from view.

Simple shapes and plain colours are however much easier to work with than vases with intricate patterns or a mixture of bright colours. If you only have room for a few vases, stick to simple shapes and plain shades such as off-white, grey, green and pewter.

If you are fortunate enough to have some lovely antique vases with flowers and other decoration painted on them, use simple arrangements that pick up the colours on the vase and either harmonise or contrast boldly with the pattern.

Baskets

There is a wide variety of attractive baskets available on the market today. They are usually made from rattan and cane and are imported from around the world. Willow baskets are more substantial but look heavier.

Baskets make a lovely, natural base for cottage-style arrangements. Mixed spring or summer flowers in small square, oblong or round baskets on the dining or side table can brighten up a room. A larger basket used in the hallway is pretty and looks very welcoming. A basket filled with a mixture of fruit or vegetables and flowers adds a homely touch to family rooms and the kitchen.

Most baskets have no lining, so a container needs to be placed inside them. Alternatively, it is possible to put stems straight into one of the varieties of water-retaining florist's foams wrapped in polythene.

Metal containers

Silver, copper, brass, pewter and bronze containers can provide the ideal shapes and colours to enhance many arrangements. Junk shops and auctions can often provide all sorts of special 'finds'.

Silver is bright and shiny and can compete for attention with some flowers but looks particularly good with greys, soft mauves and pinks. It can provide a formal elegance for a single bloom such as a rose or orchid. Always clean silver after use and take care if you have to use wire netting for your arrangement as this could scratch the surface. Try lining the container with foil, plastic or brown paper to avoid this problem.

Flowers last well in pewter containers and there are many old jugs and mugs with good simple shapes which are practical for arrangements.

The burnished shine of copper and brass containers is ideal to enhance the colour of flowers with yellow, orange and cream hues. Old copper looks particularly attractive with autumn shades. Brass is very pretty with

creams and bright greens.

Keep brass and copper clean and free from water marks. Bad stains can be removed with salt and lemon or salt and vinegar. Rub the surface hard, rinse off and dry thoroughly.

Terracotta

The variety of terracotta containers available on the market has grown rapidly over the last few years. Flower pots, troughs and urns make unusual and charming vases for cottage flower arrangements. You will need to use a waterproof container inside the terracotta receptacle, or florist's foam soaked in water and wrapped in plastic material. For an outside dining area or conservatory nothing can be more pleasing than terracotta to offset a simple one-colour arrangement.

Plastic

Many people hate plastic containers with fresh flowers but for some occasions they can be ideal. They are cheap and practical and come in every colour of the rainbow. Off-white and earth colours will be the least distracting. Bright colours would look cheerful on the table for a children's party with a simple bunch of daisies, marigolds or anemones.

Wooden containers

The natural patterns and tones of wood can provide an effective backdrop for a cottage-style arrangement.

Wooden bowls, boxes, barrels and tubs can all be useful containers. A waterproof lining is however necessary.

Baskets and terracotta pots can provide useful alternative containers to suit different styles.

BASIC EQUIPMENT
Secateurs and scissors

Sharp secateurs and a pair of short-bladed florist's scissors are essential equipment and well worth investing in. Ordinary scissors tend to squash the stems of flowers.

Florist's scissors are designed to make it easy to get right into an arrangement to snip off non-essential material. They can also be used for cutting thin wire.

A good pair of secateurs will be used constantly for gathering flowers and cutting woody branches from the garden.

Basic equipment can include secateurs, scissors, containers, plant spray, hammer, tape, wire netting, florist's foam and a craft knife.

*Stunning
colours and
shapes make
a glorious
display.*

Crumple wire into several layers in the container you are going to use.

continuously bending and folding the wire which will crack the galvanizing, causing the wire to rust and deteriorate rapidly. Place the netting so that the cut ends are at the top of the vase. They can then be twisted to clip around the rim or vase handle to hold the wire firmly in place.

To use wire in a glass container, make a tangle of netting to fill the upper third of the vase, hooking the cut ends over the rim of the glass. Then when you make your arrangement, hide this with downward-curving foliage.

If you are using a valuable china vase or silver container, either line it first with thick brown paper or try plastic-coated wire netting to avoid surface scratching.

Pinholders

These are available in many shapes and sizes with metal or plastic spikes to hold the

Wire netting

A fairly pliable chicken wire with a large mesh, approximately 5cm (2 inches), is useful. It can be bought in convenient lengths from hardware shops.

The beauty of wire as a base is that you will be able to achieve open, airy arrangements easily and can economise on the amount of material required. Keep the netting clean and dry when not in use. The amount you will need depends on the sizes and shapes of the vases you frequently use. Fold the netting into layers so that the holes overlap and stalks can be held in position at several levels. In a tall container you should aim to get four or five layers. In a shallow dish three to four layers should be enough. Once you have achieved the right shape for a particular vase, keep it only for that purpose. This avoids

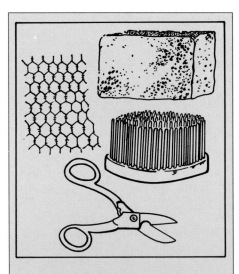

A pinholder, florist's foam, wire and florist's scissors are all useful tools.

flower stems. They are valuable for shallow containers and for flowers with thick stems.

You will probably find that you will generally use a pinholder in combination with a little wire netting. This provides weight and support for any thin-stemmed flowers in an arrangement.

Keep pinholders dry when not in use. Split thick, woody material before trying to secure it, to avoid bending the pins.

There are also small, four-pronged, plastic spikes available which can be used to anchor florist's foam to the base of containers with modelling clay.

Sand and moss

Sand can be used to set posies of flowers in small containers. It is heavy and inclined to scratch the surface of china, so only use sand with care.

Moss is an excellent medium. Use it to cover areas of soil in a planted dish or to hide an expanse of netting when arranging early spring flowers in a basket. Always soak moss in water overnight before use.

Florist's foam

Water-retaining florist's foam is useful in containers that would otherwise be too shallow to hold sufficient water. Stems will remain in place with the aid of this material; it is more difficult to achieve a natural look to an arrangement. Florists find that this material often forms a particularly useful base as it allows for easy transportation with a minimum of movement and water spillage.

After foam is cut to fit a container, it needs to be steeped in water until it is thoroughly saturated. Remember to top it up with water regularly once it is in position.

Sticky tape

Sticky tape can provide good support for

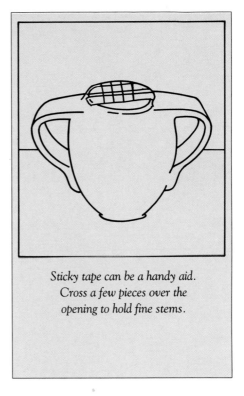

Sticky tape can be a handy aid.
Cross a few pieces over the
opening to hold fine stems.

fine foliage and is a practical support system when using glass containers.

Simply cross a few pieces of clear tape across the centre of the container and then towards the back.

Decorative stones

Pebbles, marbles and shells can all be used effectively to hold stems in glass containers, to conceal a pinholder or wire netting base.

Plant sprays

To keep flowers fresh and crisp for a longer period, a fine spray of water from above helps.

Plastic spray containers can be bought at most hardware stores or supermarkets. Alternatively, look for ornamental sprays at gift shops and flower shops.

STARTING WORK

BUYING FLOWERS can be costly but these days many people do not have their own supply. If you need a large quantity, try to visit your local flower market. These are generally open early in the morning and, apart from offering fresh flowers at extremely competitive prices, they can also be very entertaining.

SELECTING FLOWERS

Before selecting any material, look at the foliage and at the base of the stems. Discoloration can indicate age.

Flowers should look as fresh and healthy as possible with no evidence of wilting. The scent will tell you if the material has spent some length of time in water. The base of the stems should not be at all slimy.

Material selected from a florist will sometimes have been kept in cool, controlled, conditions and this will have helped to preserve them.

Flowers and foliage offered by street traders will have been subject to the effects of the prevailing weather.

Flowers such as irises, daffodils, gladioli and tulips should be bought when they are still in bud as they will soon open in a warm

Herbs growing on a window sill can provide material for an attractive flower arrangement.

room. Look for roses that have nice plump buds with good fresh foliage right up the stem. Chrysanthemums and other single, daisy-type flowers should have a hard, green centre with a ring of pollen showing yellow at the base of the petals. Poppies open very quickly in water, so if possible buy them with only a trace of colour showing.

Opposite: Growing summer flowers in a riot of colours can provide interesting material for arrangements.

*Dainty
pink roses
in a pretty
container*

WILD FLOWERS

It can be great fun to go walking in the country and gather material to bring home. Much that can be found is very attractive and you can devise some stunning arrangements. However, be aware of any local conservation rules that apply to your area and laws that protect some species.

Botanical gardens and National Parks are out of bounds and you could incur a hefty fine if you try to break the rules.

As many country plants have become quite scarce in some areas, it is very important to pick material with care. Never take the whole plant. Only cut what you need and, if your source is a small group, only take one or two pieces.

When you plan your trip to the country, take a large polythene bag lined with damp newspaper and a pair of scissors or secateurs with you. When you have cut your material, place it on the paper as quickly as possible, seal the bag and keep it in a cool place.

GARDEN FLOWERS

Growing your own flowers or foliage can provide many hours of pleasure. If you have only a small area it may pay to concentrate on growing foliage plants and supplement this constant source of material with blooms from the market or from the shops.

Preferably, cut your plants early in the morning or in the early evening when it is cooler. Carry a bucket of water with you and immediately a stem is cut, place it in the bucket. Do not gather material and leave it on the ground to be collected later as the stems will become dehydrated and cause the flowers to wilt.

Always do your cutting with secateurs or a good pair of sharp scissors. Make a clean cut and never tug at the material or you could loosen the whole plant and cause it to die.

When you have brought your material inside, leave it to stand in the bucket for several hours so that it has a long drink before arranging it in other containers.

Opposite: Flowers in profusion are a glorious sight in a florist's shop.

TECHNIQUES OF THE CRAFT

ONCE CUT, FLOWERS and FOLIAGE last for varying amounts of time. Learning some techniques which can help extend the life of your material is well worthwhile.

Whether you have obtained your material straight from the garden or from a flower shop, it should be properly treated before being arranged.

CARING FOR FLOWERS

Some general points for the care of cut flowers should be kept in mind:

- Always use containers that have been thoroughly cleaned before use.
- Always use clean water.
- Put material into water as soon as possible after cutting and leave it overnight in a cool place before arranging.
- Any material that has wilted should initially be soaked in warm water.
- Cut all stems at an angle so that if they slip to the bottom of a containers they do not sit flat on the base where dirt can then prevent the intake of moisture.
- Remove broken stems or leaves and thin-out unwanted shoots.
- Remove all foliage which will be below the water line.
- Spray the air over the material with a fine mist of water to charge it with moisture.
- Never attempt to open flowers with your fingers or by any other device.
- Do not place flowers in direct heat or in direct sunlight.
- Keep flowers out of draughts.

Cut flower stems at an angle.

Opposite: Flower stems can be treated in different ways to prolong their life.
The hard, woody stem of the protea, on the left, has been split. The gerbera stem is cut at an angle.
The rose stem has been cut at an angle and dipped in boiling water.
The stem of the eucalyptus has also been dipped in boiling water
and crushed with a hammer to break up the fibres.

Nowadays it is possible to buy a proprietary chemical substance which extends the life of some flowers. Use these materials according to the manufacturer's instructions.

Over the years some discoveries have been made which, although not based on scientific fact, are known to help extend the life of some plants. It is certainly no old wives's tale that aspirin helps to keep flowers fresh and that flowers are known to last well in metal containers. A copper coin in water slows down the breeding rate of bacteria and a few drops of weak disinfectant will help to keep the water the flowers are in smelling fresh.

TREATING STEMS

Soft stems

Flowers with soft, succulent stems, for example, tulips, arum lilies and clivia should have their stems cut at an angle and be placed immediately in deep water. Some flowers from this particular group exude a slimy sap. Hyacinths and narcissi come into this category. Place those types of flowers in water on their own for an hour or so and then put them into fresh clean water.

Tulips also require additional care to bring out the best from them. Cut their soft stems at an angle and if they are thick, split them at the base for about 1cm (3/8 inch). Remove the bottom leaves and then, before placing them in deep, tepid water for a long drink, bunch them together with their heads level and roll them in grease-proof paper just covering the flower heads. This will stop the heads falling forward and breaking off.

Hard, woody stems

Plants that fall into this category should have their stems cut at an angle and then split with a pair of secateurs, or hammered to

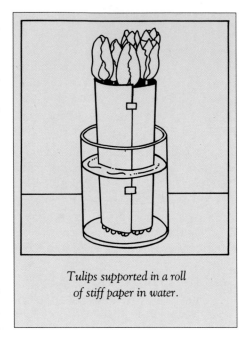

Tulips supported in a roll of stiff paper in water.

break up the fibres. If a stem is particularly woody, 2.5cm (3/4 inch) of bark should be stripped from its base before hammering so that the white stem beneath the bark shows clearly. Remove unwanted foliage and stems. Place the material into a deep bucket of water initially.

If there is a time delay between cutting and placing the material into water in its final receptacle, dip the tips of the stems in hot water for a few minutes first and then stand in warm water.

Stems which bleed

When some flowers are picked, a white ring of thick, milky sap forms on the cut surface. Either place the tips of the stems of these plants in shallow boiling water for controlled, 30 seconds or singe the cut tip in a candle flame for a few seconds.

Roses

Remove all the thorns from a rose by rubbing with the back of a pair of secateurs or cutting them from the stem. The exception to this treatment is for the single rose which is going to be displayed in a specimen vase. Excess foliage should also be removed straightaway. Place roses into deep water, but if they are limp, they should be wrapped in a roll of stiff paper first to support the heads.

There are two ways to revive roses that have started to wilt, provided the flower head has not fallen so far to one side that it has cracked the stem tissue. The first is to re-cut the rose stem and split it, place the tip in boiling water for 30 seconds, then wrap the stem and flower in stiff paper and place the stem in lukewarm water for a long drink.

Alternatively, re-cut the stems and submerge the flower and stem in a bath of water for a couple of hours.

Smelly stems

If you want to use a flower or foliage that is known to smell in water, it is best to isolate it from other material. One way is to wrap the cut stem in wet cottonwool which has been dipped in disinfectant and secure the stem in a polythene bag with a rubber band before putting it with the other material.

Hollow stems

Flowers with hollow stems require special treatment as it is difficult for water to get to the flower head. After cutting, turn the flower upside down and fill the stalk with water. Seal the end with your finger until you have placed it in deep water.

FINISHING TECHNIQUES

THERE ARE A VARIETY OF BOOKS, paintings, pictures and calendars available which will give you lots of inspiration when it comes to arranging flowers in your home. Study these carefully; decide if the arrangement is suitable for the location you have in mind; check whether the material will be readily available or if you can adapt the arrangement to suit the flowers and foliage in your garden.

The character of your home and the

Individual arrangements for each guest at a dining table look pretty.

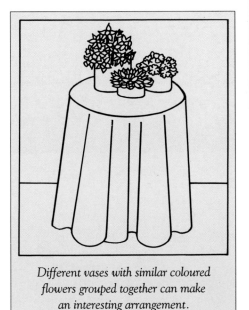

Different vases with similar coloured flowers grouped together can make an interesting arrangement.

particular room where you want to put flowers will dictate the style of arrangement you are looking for. Consider the type of furnishings you have, the colours in the room and where the flowers will be placed.

Generally, people aim for one or two fairly large arrangements in a room. However, do not overlook smaller arrangements grouped together or placed on a table in conjunction with other complimentary items perhaps of a similar colour.

Dining table arrangements do not have to

Opposite: A table setting is enhanced by a simple arrangement of tulips.

A mixture of herbs and flowers can make an unusual and attractive table arrangement.

be restricted to one formal piece in the centre of the table. Individual nosegays placed in front of each guest work well. Herbs offer another range of decorative options with the addition of an attractive scent. They can be used in bunches, on their own or mixed with flowers.

Arranging flowers is a creative art. No two arrangements will turn out to be exactly the same which is part of the fun of this particular craft. Experiment with different types of flowers and foliage and different sized arrangements until you develop your own individual style.

Often people tend to have one particular place in a room where they always put their flowers. Try breaking this habit and experiment with different locations.

BASIC SHAPE

When you study most flower arrangements, you will readily discern that they are based on a triangular shape. Even when an arrangement is quite casual and loose, the underlying structure is still usually the triangle.

The triangle is a simple design and once mastered will provide you with the basis for all sorts of beautiful arrangements. It consists of different flowers serving three separate functions.

First, choose a selection of flowers and foliage to form the basic outline of the arrangement.

Secondly, add your focal flowers towards the centre of the arrangement. These should form a focal point to which the eye is drawn and should step down from one flower to the next from top to bottom.

Finally, add smaller flowers to fill in between the focal flowers and the outline.

Practise with this basic shape until you feel confident with it and then experiment using it as a base only. You will soon develop your own individual ideas which will provide you with the style you most like.

Step 1 *Form the basic outline.*

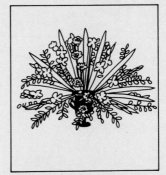

Step 2 *Add your focal flowers.*

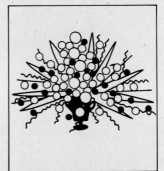

Step 3 *Add small flowers (represented by black dots) to fill out the arrangement.*

*Terracotta pots are grouped together
to create a mantelpiece arrangement.
The candles have been held in
place by moss.*

The triangle provides the basic shape for this pretty arrangement for the Christmas table made with flowers, cones and sparkling novelties.

Christmas provides the opportunity to experiment with fresh and dried flowers and accessories of all shapes and sizes.

Right   *Wrong*

*Soften the rim of a container with a few leaves
to avoid a stiff, unnatural look.*

GENERAL TIPS

- Before beginning work, place the vase you are going to use in its final position and try to arrange the flowers at the height where they are to stand.

  Raising or lowering a vase after an arrangement has been completed can dramatically alter its appearance.

- Try to find flowers in their various stages of growth.

  Mix buds with half-open flowers.

- Flower stems need to be of different lengths to avoid a flat appearance.

  To begin with, keep larger flowers of deeper colours for the centre or focal point of the arrangement.

- Look at your arrangement from the side as well as from the front to check that it has a balanced look.

- Point a few stems slightly backwards for balance and style.

- All the stems in the arrangement should radiate from a centre point. Try to achieve a natural look in the finished arrangement.

- Allow some of your material to come over the front and sides of the container to break any hard lines.

- If you are only using one or two colours and kinds of flowers, group them close together for impact.

*Opposite: This shallow, black dish contains a piece of florist's foam covered with moss.
Anemones have been arranged to provide a colourful display.*

BEGINNER'S PROJECT

Designed by Wendy B.

THE PROJECT WHICH HAS BEEN designed for you to complete is a charming exercise, simple to master and adaptable for use on a variety of items.

In the illustrations, we have shown how a few flowers, scissors and small florist's foam shape (readily available from florists and floral supply shops) can be used to create an individual flower arrangement to decorate napkin rings for that special meal.

Before starting work, consider carefully the colours you should use to enhance the presentation of your dinner table.

Read through all the instructions and then gather together the material you need.

MATERIALS

You will need the following items:

- A napkin ring for each place setting.
- The same number of small florist's foam shapes. These should have a self-adhesive tab on the back to attach the napkin ring when the arrangement is complete.
- Scissors.
- Some small-leafed foliage to form the outline.
- Focal flowers. For our example we have used small pink roses.
- Filling/outline flowers. These should be tiny. We have used sweet peas and gypsophila.
- Napkin.
- Paper towels

Opposite: The completed arrangement looks delightful and would adorn any table setting.

Example of how the base leaves and outline flowers are arranged to cover the florist's foam shape.

METHOD

Step One

Float the foam shapes upside down in water until they are thoroughly soaked. Remove them and immediately wipe off any drops on the underside with a paper towel so that the sticky pad does not get wet.

Step Two

Select your small-leafed foliage and cut it into lengths of approximately 5cm (2 inches). Remove any bottom leaves that prevent you sliding the stem into the shape. Push the stems gently into the shape to form a ring right around the base.

Cut your outline flowers to approximately 5cm (2 inches) too. Removing any leaves, push them into the shape so that it is evenly covered.

Add your focal flowers towards the centre of the arrangement.

Finally, fill any remaining spaces with more outline flowers either of a similar or contrasting shade to match your table decor.

Step Three

Roll your napkin into a long cylinder and thread it through the napkin ring.

Peel the cover from the sticky pad on the foam shape and carefully press it onto the napkin ring.

Voilà! You have the perfect decorative touch for your next dinner party.

Experiment with different arrangements on the florist's foam shape to easily adapt this project and attach it to a range of gifts for birthdays, Mothering Sunday, Christmas or any other special occasion.

Our charming beginner's project easily adapts to different arrangements for use on gifts.

INDEX